Published by Creative Education
and Creative Paperbacks
P.O. Box 227, Mankato, Minnesota 56002
Creative Education and Creative Paperbacks
are imprints of The Creative Company
www.thecreativecompany.us

Design by The Design Lab
Production by Travis Green
Art direction by Rita Marshall
Printed in the United States of America

Photographs by Alamy (Arco Images GmbH, Juniors
Bildarchiv GmbH), Corbis (Ingo Arndt/Minden
Pictures, DLILLC, Charles Krebs, Claus Meyer/Minden
Pictures), Dreamstime (Isselee), Getty Images (altrendo
nature, STEVE MASLOWSKI), Newscom (Andy Rouse/
NHPA/Photoshot), Shutterstock (Cynthia Kidwell, Ryan
Morgan), SuperStock (Animals Animals)

Library of Congress Cataloging-in-Publication Data
Bodden, Valerie.
Skunks / Valerie Bodden.
p. cm. — (Amazing animals)
Summary: A basic exploration of the appearance,
behavior, and habitat of skunks, the musk-spraying
mammals. Also included is a story from folklore
explaining the unpleasant scent of skunks.
Includes bibliographical references and index.
ISBN 978-1-60818-614-3 (hardcover)
ISBN 978-1-62832-220-0 (pbk)
ISBN 978-1-56660-661-5 (eBook)
1. Skunks—Juvenile literature. I. Title. II. Series:
Amazing animals.
QL737.C248B63 2016
599.76'8—dc23   2014048707

CCSS: RI.1.1, 2, 4, 5, 6, 7; RI.2.2, 5, 6, 7, 10;
RI.3.1, 5, 7, 8; RF.1.1, 3, 4; RF.2.3, 4

First Edition HC 9 8 7 6 5 4 3 2 1
First Edition PBK 9 8 7 6 5 4 3 2 1

AMAZING ANIMALS

SKUNKS

BY VALERIE BODDEN

CREATIVE EDUCATION • CREATIVE PAPERBACKS

Skunks use their senses of smell and hearing to explore

Skunks are **mammals**. They squirt a stinky liquid called musk. There are 12 kinds of skunks in the world.

mammals animals that have hair or fur and feed their babies with milk

The most common skunks have a black body with white stripes. But some skunks are black with white spots. Skunks have long, fluffy tails, short legs, and big feet. Sharp claws help them dig.

Some skunks have fur that looks brown or gray

Most skunks are about the size of a pet cat. But some are smaller. The smallest skunks weigh only about two pounds (0.9 kg).

The eastern spotted skunk weighs 0.5 to 2 pounds (0.2–0.9 kg)

*Striped skunks live
in the United States,
Canada, and Mexico*

Skunks are found mainly on the **continents** of North and South America. They can live in forests, grasslands, and **mountains**. Some skunks even live in cities!

continents Earth's seven big pieces of land

mountains very big hills made of rock

Some skunks raid turkey nests to steal the large eggs

Skunks will eat almost anything. Their favorite foods are **grubs** and insects. But they will also eat worms, mice, and bird eggs. Skunks eat berries, nuts, and corn, too. They even eat garbage!

grubs short, fat, white worms that grow to become insects

A mother skunk gives birth to four to six **kits**. At first, the kits have no fur. They cannot hear or see. But they drink their mother's milk and grow. When they are seven weeks old, their mother teaches them how to find food. The kits leave their mother when they are about five months old. Most skunks live three or four years.

kits baby skunks

Skunks spend most of the day sleeping in their dens, or homes. Many skunks make their dens in hollow logs. At night, skunks come out to hunt. Skunks usually live and hunt alone.

Many skunks hunt all night and return to their dens at sunrise

*A skunk raises its tail
and arches its back
before it sprays*

Sometimes a predator

like a fox comes near a skunk. The skunk hisses and stomps. If that doesn't scare the fox, the skunk sprays it with musk. The musk hurts the predator's skin and eyes.

predator an animal that kills and eats other animals

Many people see—or smell—skunks in the wild. Some people even keep skunks as pets. Usually pet skunks have their **scent glands** removed. As long as you are not getting sprayed, it can be fun to watch these smelly animals!

scent glands the parts of a skunk's body that make musk

A *Skunk Story*

Why do skunks smell bad? American Indians told a story about this. They said that Skunk was once as big as an elephant. But Fox was jealous of Skunk's black-and-white coat. He asked the **medicine man** to give him Skunk's coat. Without his coat, Skunk was smaller than the other animals. But another medicine man gave Skunk a way to protect himself—his smell.

medicine man a person believed to have special healing powers

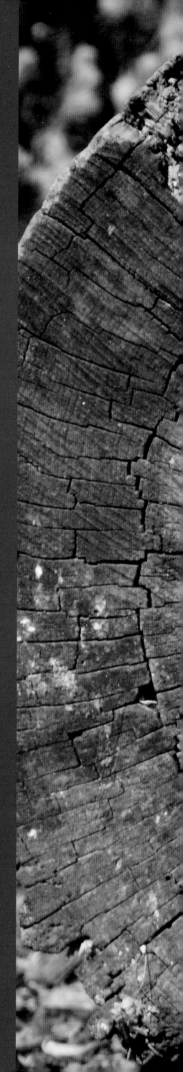

Read More

FitzSimmons, David. *Curious Critters*. Vol. 2. Bellville, Ohio: Wild Iris, 2014.

Green, Emily. *Skunks*. Minneapolis: Bellwether Media, 2011.

Websites

Enchanted Learning: Striped Skunk
http://www.enchantedlearning.com/subjects/mammals/skunk/Skunkcoloring.shtml
This site has skunk facts and a picture to color.

National Geographic Kids: Skunks
http://kids.nationalgeographic.com/content/kids/en_US/animals/skunk/
Learn lots more skunk facts.

Note: Every effort has been made to ensure that the websites listed above are suitable for children, that they have educational value, and that they contain no inappropriate material. However, because of the nature of the Internet, it is impossible to guarantee that these sites will remain active indefinitely or that their contents will not be altered.

Index